Community Helpers

School Principals

by Tracey Boraas

Consultant:
Sidney Morrison, President
Association of California School Administrators

Bridgestone Books
an imprint of Capstone Press
Mankato, Minnesota

Bridgestone Books are published by Capstone Press
151 Good Counsel Drive, P.O. Box 669, Mankato, MN 56002
http://www.capstone-press.com

Library of Congress Cataloging-in-Publication Data
Boraas, Tracey.
    School principals/by Tracey Boraas.
    p. cm.—(Community helpers)
    Includes bibliographical references and index.
    Summary: A simple introduction to the clothing, tools, schooling, and work of school
principals.
    ISBN 0-7368-0074-3
    1. School principals—Juvenile literature. 2. School management and organization—
Juvenile literature. [1. School principals. 2. Occupations.] I. Title. II. Series: Community
helpers (Mankato, Minn.)
LB2831.9.B67 1999
371.2'012—DC21   98-18471
                                                              CIP
                                                              AC

Editorial Credits
Michael Fallon, editor; James Franklin, cover designer; Sheri Gosewisch, photo researcher

Photo Credits
Don Franklin, 16
Frank S. Balthis, 6, 12
James L. Shaffer, cover, 20
Leslie O'Shaughnessy, 18
Photo Network/Jay Thomas, 4
Ulrich Tutsch, 10
Unicorn Stock Photos/D & I MacDonald, 8; Chromosohm/Sohm, 14

2 3 4 5 6 06 05 04 03 02

Table of Contents

School Principals

School principals are leaders of schools. They make important decisions about school business. School principals help teachers teach children. Principals make sure schools are safe places.

What School Principals Do

School principals do many jobs. They hire teachers to work in schools. Principals sometimes help teachers decide what to teach. Principals make safety rules for schools too.

Where School Principals Work

School principals work at elementary schools. They also work at middle schools and high schools. Principals meet with parents, students, and teachers in school offices. Principals visit school classrooms and playgrounds throughout the day.

Tools School Principals Use

School principals use computers to look at tests and test scores. Principals use test results to find better ways for students to learn. Principals use telephones to talk to people about school business. They write notes to students, teachers, and parents.

School Principals and Teachers

School principals and teachers sometimes work together. They think about what students need to learn. They plan lessons together. Principals and teachers think of better ways to teach lessons.

School Principals and Training

People must study in colleges to become school principals. They go to college after finishing high school. These college students learn how to teach children. They study school business. They also learn to be good leaders.

School Principals and Communities

School principals talk to communities about schools. Principals tell people about school business and how well students are doing. They also ask communities to help schools. Principals want to make schools better places for students to learn.

People Who Help School Principals

Secretaries help school principals by doing office work. They help plan principals' work days. Assistant principals also help school principals. They aid principals with school business.

How School Principals Help Others

School principals care about students and teachers. Principals work hard to help students learn. They help teachers plan lessons for students. Principals also make sure schools are safe places to learn.

Hands on: Help Students Learn

School principals help students learn. They help students find answers to problems. You can help students find answers when playing an alphabet game.

What You Need

A group of friends

What You Do

1. Choose one person to be the principal. Everyone else should stand in a circle around the principal.
2. The principal must choose a subject such as animals. The principal tells a player to name an animal that begins with A. The next player then names an animal that begins with B. Players continue through the rest of the alphabet.
3. The principal should help players who cannot think of answers. The principal can give these players hints.
4. After finishing the alphabet, the principal chooses a new player to be principal. The new principal chooses a different subject. Some other subjects are foods, jobs, and countries. Continue playing the game until everyone has been the principal.

Words to Know

assistant (uh-SISS-tuhnt)—a person who helps someone else do a job

college (KOL-ij)—a school where students study after high school

lesson (LESS-uhn)—a set of facts that students learn in school

secretary (SEK-ruh-ter-ee)—a person who does office work

Read More

Deedrick, Tami. *Teachers.* Community Helpers. Mankato, Minn.: Capstone Press, 1998.

Grant, Jim and Irv Richardson. *What Principals Do When No One Is Looking.* Peterborough, N.H.: Crystal Springs Books, 1998.

Internet Sites

Edunet Connect
http://www.edunetconnect.com/index_e.html
National Association of Elementary School Principals
http://www.naesp.org

Index